Understanding
My Terrapin

Reptiles are becoming very popular pets and are overtaking cats and dogs as household members, however, their husbandry requirements are much more complex to keep them happy and healthy.

As a company who sees every day the shortfalls in caring for these specialised animals, we are pleased to endorse the series of "Reptiles are Cool" written by Siuna Reid, an experienced exotic veterinarian who cares enough to try and make a difference.

These books are very basic and provide simple steps and explanations of how and why we need to provide specialised environments for our pet reptiles to improve their captive quality of life as best we can.

—Pinmoore Animal Laboratory Services

REPTILES ARE COOL

Understanding
My Terrapin

Siuna A Reid
BVMS Cert AVP (ZM) MRCVS

Edited by
Vivienne E Lodge

CONTENTS

Siuna A Reid

INTRODUCTION

I have been a vet for a long time and I have seen many changes in the kinds of animals that I treat. Over the past ten years there has been a huge increase in the number of reptiles that are kept as pets.

Reptiles are very different from mammals. The purpose of this book is to try to explain these differences and why they are important to the health and wellbeing of pet reptiles.

There are many different species of terrapins that are kept as pets. The onus is on the supervising adult to research the specific requirements before buying their pet. This book explains the importance of husbandry and some of the diseases that can occur if basic needs are not fulfilled.

Later in the book you will come across the following symbols. Each one highlights a particular aspect of your reptile's care, relating directly to the health issue being discussed.

Reptiles carry many different bacteria, one of which is salmonella. Although not harmful to them, the bacteria can cause illness in humans. Therefore, it is essential to wash your hands thoroughly after handling all reptiles.

House

Furniture

Heat and Light

UV light

Water/Humidity

Food

TERRAPINS AS PETS

Buying a pet and looking after it is a huge responsibility. As a pet owner you have to make sure that your pet has somewhere suitable to live, has the correct food to eat and receives lots of care and attention. You must notice when your pet is not feeling well and needs to be taken to the vet.

The most commonly kept pets are mammals such as dogs, cats, rabbits and hamsters. Humans are mammals too, so we generally find it quite easy to relate to other mammals and to realise when they are unwell or in distress. If you stand on your dog's paw he will yelp and you will know he is in pain. If your dog is too cold you will notice that he is shivering and if he is too hot you will notice him panting. If he doesn't eat his dinner you will realise that he is feeling unwell.

You have chosen to keep a terrapin as a pet. Terrapins are reptiles and reptiles are very different from mammals. Your terrapin will not give you such obvious signals to let you know that he is feeling unwell, too hot, too cold, or in pain. His signs of distress are much more subtle and you will have to observe him very closely to make sure that he remains healthy in order to prevent any suffering going unnoticed. You should weigh your terrapin regularly as it may not be obvious from just looking at him that he is losing weight.

Many of the health problems which occur in terrapins are related to some aspect of their environment or their diet. In this book we will first look at the correct housing and feeding for your terrapin. Then we will go through the body systems of your terrapin to find out how they work and what to look out for should things go wrong.

3

CAPTIVE BRED

Wherever possible buy a captive bred terrapin. Terrapins bought from wild stock are often exposed to, and can carry a wide range of different parasites, bacteria and viruses. Buying a wild caught terrapin also encourages this unethical trade.

CITES PROTECTION

A CITES certificate is issued to protect endangered species and enables the tracking of all animals with the certificate. Be sure to check if your terrapin needs a certificate. Certain species of terrapin must have a CITES if they are to be bought or sold.

Some terrapins are captive bred in other countries and then imported to Britain. Once the terrapin has grown to a length greater than 10cm, it must have a microchip placed in its leg. A form is completed and sent to the CITES board. It is illegal to sell or buy these terrapins without a microchip and certificate.

HOLIDAY CARE

Everybody needs a holiday! When choosing a suitable place for your terrapin to stay whilst you are away, ensure that he is not exposed to other terrapins. If your terrapin is either living in isolation, or in an isolated group, suddenly placing him in an environment where there are other terrapins is dangerous. There is a huge risk of disease spread. Wherever possible, arrange for your terrapin to be cared for at your own home.

INSURANCE

There are not many pets that potentially have a life expectancy similar to our own. It is possible that you may have to make provisions for your terrapin in your will! Please remember that terrapin care is specialised and should they

4

become ill treatment can be expensive. Insurance is one way to protect your terrapin.

HIBERNATION

Many species of terrapins are able to hibernate but it is not essential as it is for tortoises. Hibernation is a way of escaping weather or conditions that are too poor to live in. Some terrapins hibernate to avoid very hot weather and others hibernate to escape very cold weather.

VISITING THE VET

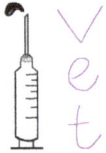

At some point you may need to take your terrapin to the vet. This symbol, which you will come across throughout the book, indicates when you may need to seek extra help, medicine or maybe even surgery for your terrapin. Try to choose a vet who has a special interest in reptiles. Some vets take more exams so that they have extra qualifications for treating reptiles. If your local vets are not reptile enthusiasts they should be able to recommend a vet who is. If you have difficulty finding a suitable vet you could contact The Royal College of Veterinary Surgeons www.rcvs.org.uk.

THE HOUSE

Where will your terrapin live? You will need to buy a tank for him. It is best to get the house (and also the things that you put in it – see below) from a specialist reptile shop. Tanks made of glass or plastic are a good idea as these materials are easy to clean.

Within the tank you need to try and create a small world which mimics the kind of environment your type of terrapin would exist in if it were in the wild. Therefore it is very important that you fully research your chosen species so that you can create the correct living environment.

Terrapins live in water but must have dry land to be able to bask in the sun. A tank with water and an area with rocks or a built in basking area need to be included within the house.

It is also important to think about where you will place the terrapin's house in your own home. The best place to place it is in a room that is used, like your bedroom or the main living room. Your terrapin needs to be somewhere with a constant temperature. Do not put his house beside a window or over a radiator as the temperature will rise and fall too much in these areas.

SUBSTRATE & FURNITURE

Substrate is the material used to cover the floor of your terrapin's house. Gravel that is used for fish tanks is suitable to cover the floor of the house. You will also need to place some furniture. He needs to have somewhere to hide, especially if his house is in a busy room. You can buy him a plastic cave or you can use pieces of wood or small logs to make a hide.

HEAT AND LIGHT

Life on Earth is supported by the sun. The sun provides heat and also light. Animals need both heat and light to survive.

Mammals can control their own body temperature. The food they eat provides the body with energy and heat. If they are too cold they shiver and if they are too hot they sweat. These processes use a lot of energy.

Your terrapin is a reptile and reptiles regulate their body temperature very differently from mammals. This is a major and vitally important difference. Reptiles are cold blooded (exothermic). This means that their bodies cannot produce heat from the food that they eat. Because of this they need much less energy from food to survive. A 100g reptile needs only 5% of the energy that a 100g mammal needs. To keep warm they need to bathe in the sun or sit on a warm rock. They have no hair, no sweat glands and do not shiver. This means that your terrapin will show no obvious signs that they are too hot or too cold.

You need to provide sources of heat for your terrapin within his house. This could be a heat bulb, a ceramic bulb or an under floor heating mat. It is important that you know the temperature in your terrapin's house, both the hottest and the coolest areas. To do this you will need to use thermometers in their house.

If you are not aware of the temperature in your terrapin's house there is a danger that he could become too hot. As he cannot sweat to cool off or remove layers of clothing as we would, he will need to try to hide in a cooler part of his tank.

It is more common however, for a terrapin to find himself in an environment which is too cold. Cooler temperatures are unlikely to kill him but will put a strain on his body and organs. His muscles, lungs, intestines and heart will struggle to work if they are too cold. If this goes on for a long time it can lead to illness and even death.

ULTRA VIOLET LIGHT

As well as producing heat and light the sun also produces ultraviolet (UV) light. This is a type of light which we cannot see but terrapins can. It affects the skin and in humans it can cause sunburn.

Reptiles use UV light to make vitamin D3. This helps to keep their bones strong and healthy and enables their intestines to absorb calcium from their food. To obtain vitamin D3 he will need exposure to UV light for 12 hours a day.

If your terrapin does not receive enough vitamin D3 his shell may become soft and spongy. The shell and the bones act as a huge store for calcium.

Ultra violet light can be provided in the form of a combination bulb or a UV tube. The tube needs to be no more than 30cm away from your terrapin. Remember that a regular UV tube will not provide him with any heat. The bulb should be changed once a year and although it may appear to be working, over time it eventually stops producing any UV light.

In Britain there is a good source of UV light from March until September. Where possible, adult terrapins can spend time outside on sunny warm days in a suitable enclosure. However, be warned, terrapins are escape artists!

WATER

All terrapins need water to drink. Terrapins are unusual because they are one of the few pet reptiles that live in water. Water quality is important. The quality of water does not need to be to the exacting standard for keeping fish, but it is important that it is clean and regularly changed. An under gravel filter can help to keep the water free of bacteria. Feeding your terrapins in a separate container helps to reduce the amount of waste food and poo that finds its way into the water. Remember your terrapin spends a lot of time in water, so make sure it does not become a toilet! A filter is essential to help keep the water free of bacteria.

Humidity is also an important consideration when setting up your terrapin's house. When water evaporates it forms an invisible gas called water vapour. Humidity is a measure of the amount of water vapour that is present in the air.

In hot dry areas like deserts, there is very little water vapour in the air which means that deserts have low humidity. Rain forests are also hot but have lots of water vapour in the air and so they have high levels of humidity. Some species of terrapin need to have a water heater.

The level of humidity required for your terrapin will depend on what sort of terrapin he is and therefore what type of environment he needs. You can use a gadget called a hygrometer to measure the humidity levels in your terrapin's house to ensure that it is suitable for him.

FOOD

Most terrapins are omnivores. This means that they eat a diet consisting of meat, vegetable material, and specialised dried terrapin food. Some terrapins like one food more than another but it is important to make sure that the diet is varied.

In the wild, the terrapin would search and catch live food. Terrapins are true survivors and will eat a wide variety of food. In captivity, pinkies, earthworms and mealworms are readily available from pet shops. Fresh fish, prawns, and leafy vegetables can also be bought from local shops. Make sure the food is chopped to the correct size for your terrapin and a good vitamin supplement is added to the food before feeding. There are a number of commercially available dried pelleted diets. This type of food has all the correct vitamins and minerals already added.

Feeding the terrapin out of the tank also helps to reduce contamination of the water by preventing old, uneaten food falling into the water and rotting. Most terrapins will poo after eating and if trained to eat in a small tank this can also help to reduce contamination in the main house.

A good source of calcium is essential. This can easily be added by sprinkling a calcium powder over the food before feeding three times a week.

13

SKIN

The skin is the largest organ of the body. Reptile skin is unique and has many functions which include protecting the body, providing camouflage and making vitamin D3. This is a yellow eared terrapin.

SHEDDING (ECDYSIS)

Each square on the shell is called a scute.

When mammals grow their skin stretches and grows too. Reptiles are different. Their skin does not stretch with growth. Therefore, the ability to shed skin is very important to your terrapin. When it is time to shed, your terrapin will produce a chemical which divides the old and the new skin. When the legs start to shed, skin will begin to flake and come away in pieces. The shell sheds scutes. These are areas of hard skin that grow over the bones of the shell. As the terrapin grows the scutes become bigger.

A soft shelled turtle

Make sure that the temperature in your terrapin's house is correct. If it is too cold he will struggle to shed and grow.

A balanced diet is essential for the skin to remain healthy.

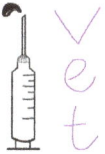

Any problems relating to shedding should be closely monitored and may require a visit to the vet.

SKIN PROBLEMS

This photo shows an abscess in the ear.

Abscesses are lumps on the skin which are infected with bacteria or fungi. Damaged skin is a common cause of infection.

Check for sharp objects in the house.

Correct temperature will help your terrapin fight off infection.

A good diet keeps the immune system healthy.

Make sure all the furniture has smooth edges

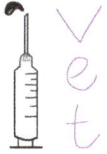

If your terrapin develops an abscess he will need to have an operation to remove it.

FLY STRIKE

A maggot

Fly strike is a condition seen mainly in terrapins that are kept outside. Any scratches or diarrhoea that remains unnoticed attracts flies like the blue and the green bottle. These lay their eggs in the damaged tissue and the larvae eat the flesh of the terrapin.

Check your terrapin daily for wounds and make sure he is clean.

A good diet prevents diarrhoea.

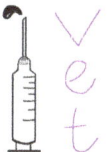

This condition needs a visit to the vet. The larvae will need to be removed and the wounds cleaned and treated with antibiotics.

17

Poor diet can affect the skin. Terrapin skin needs Vitamin A. Too little of it causes the skin of the eyes and the mouth to become swollen. Poor sight will make it very difficult to see and therefore feeding becomes a challenge.

Too much vitamin A in the diet causes the skin to become thickened and flaky.

A diet with low calcium and low vitamin D3, but with lots of fat, can result in the body growing too quickly. This leads to weak bones and skin that will shed over and over again.

To help your terrapin make vitamin D3, his UV bulb needs to have the correct strength and be in the right position. During the summer months a pen outside in the garden gives excellent exposure to UV light. Just remember it is chilly at night.

Make sure you feed a balanced diet to your terrapin to ensure he gets the correct amount of nutrients, vitamins and minerals to keep his skin healthy. Remember to dust his salad leaves with a calcium powder.

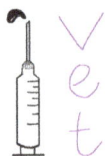

Most nutritional diseases require veterinary assistance. Your terrapin may need injections of multivitamins.

18

Terrapins are very active and will dig and scratch at the house. Damage to the skin is very common and can be serious.

Make sure there are no sharp edges in the house. Check his skin for damage.

The correct temperature in the house helps to keep the immune system healthy and speeds up the healing process.

A healthy diet is ensures the terrapin's body is kept in good condition.

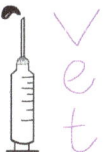

Serious damage can take a long time to heal. Antibiotics and surgery may be required to fix some wounds.

Infections of the shell are not common, however they can be very difficult to treat and can often result in large areas becoming ulcerated and therefore painful.

It is vital to make sure that the house and the furniture are in excellent condition. The shell can be damaged by poor housing. Also cage mates often bite, leading to an increased risk of infection.

The correct temperature keeps the immune system healthy and UV light keeps the shell strong and therefore less likely to become damaged.

Reducing the levels of bacteria in the water is vital. This can be done by using a biological filter and feeding the terrapin outside of the house.

Feeding a balanced diet helps to maintain the immune system.

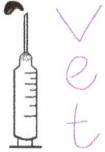

This condition may need considerable veterinary treatment which may include antibiotics and barrier creams to prevent the spread of infection.

EYES

Terrapins are thought to have excellent eyesight. Their eyelids are quite different to ours. If you look at your own eye you will see that you have a big upper eyelid which comes down to cover your eye when you blink and a much smaller lower eyelid. In terrapins the lower eyelid is the one which is bigger and stronger. This is often transparent so that the terrapin can see under water with his eyes shut. Terrapins also have a third eyelid which sweeps across the surface of the eye to clean it when they blink.

See through lower lid

The coloured circle in your eye is called the iris. This deterimines whether you have green, blue or brown eyes. The pupil is in the centre of the iris. Your pupil will be black and round. It can become bigger or smaller depending on the amount of light around you.

Terrapins have round pupils and they have tiny bones in the white part of their eyes called scleral ossicles. These help to give the eyeball extra strength.

EYE PROBLEMS

CONJUNCTIVITIS

Conjunctivitis is the inflammation of the eyelids. It is often caused by a bacterial infection.

Low temperatures in your terrapin's house will reduce his ability to fight infection.

A well balanced diet is vital to keep your terrapin healthy.

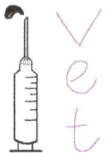

Conjunctivitis should be treated with antibiotics.

23

A diet lacking in vitamin A can lead to swelling of the eyelids.

Make sure you feed a balanced diet with enough vitamin A to prevent eye problems in your terrapin. It is important not to give too much vitamin A as this can lead to liver damage.

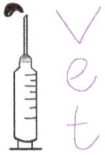

The vet may need to give your terrapin injections of vitamin A.

TRAUMA (DAMAGE)

Any trauma to your terrapin's eye could cause serious damage. This could happen in any number of ways. Examples would be, bedding caught in the eye or a scratch by a sharp object. An ulcer may form on the cornea. The cornea is the transparent outer layer of the eye. Ulcers are very painful and in severe cases the eye could burst.

To prevent eye trauma you should check your terrapin's house and furniture carefully for any sharp objects. Remember care should be taken when handling your terrapin outside of his house.

Take care when selecting a UV light for your terrapin's house. Inferior lights can emit harmful rays which could burn his eyes.

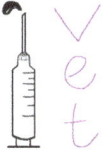

If you suspect that your terrapin has suffered trauma to his eye take him to the vet immediately. Eye damage is an emergency and if not treated in time your terrapin may lose his eye.

CONGENITAL (BIRTH) EYE DEFECTS

This picture shows a young terrapin with a normal eye on the left and a very small eye on the right. This is called micro opthalmia. The terrapin was born like this and is unlikely to have any vision in the right eye.

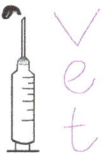

Micro opthalmia is not painful. However, the eyesight will be affected and you may notice him bumping into things. Over time it is possible that eye may become infected and may need veterinary treatment.

DIGESTIVE SYSTEM

The digestive system converts food into energy. Left over waste is expelled through the vent.

The digestive tract of your terrapin consists of the mouth, stomach, intestines and vent. The vent is the reptile equivalent of the anus in mammals.

MOUTH

Terrapins have a beak like a bird. They have no teeth. The roof of our mouth is called the hard palate. The terrapin does not have a roof to his mouth. Instead he has a hole called the choana. Terrapins have a short, fleshy and sensitive tongue.

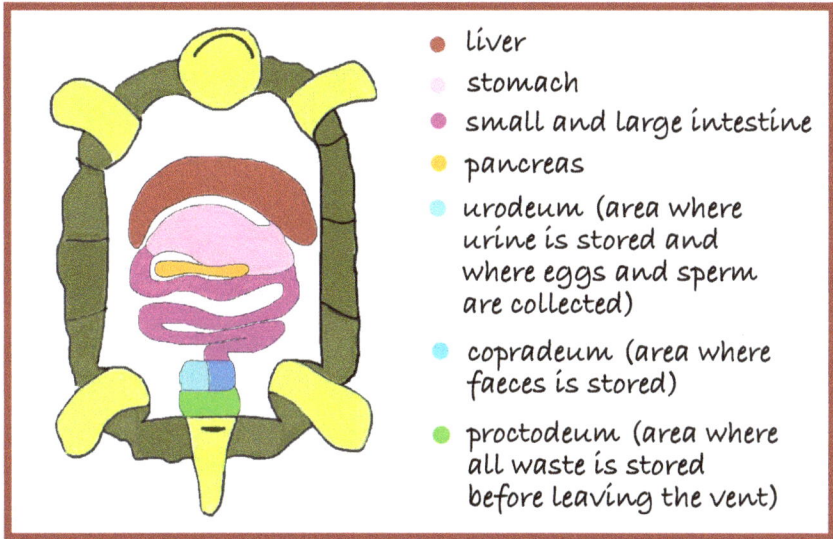

- **liver**
- stomach
- **small and large intestine**
- pancreas
- urodeum (area where urine is stored and where eggs and sperm are collected)
- copradeum (area where faeces is stored)
- **proctodeum (area where all waste is stored before leaving the vent)**

STOMACH

A tube called the oesophagus leads from the mouth to the stomach.

INTESTINES

After the stomach the digestive tract continues as the small and large intestine.

VENT

The vent is made up of three areas. The food waste from the large intestine is stored in the coprodeum. The urodeum is the area which stores urine, and also any sperm or eggs (depending on whether your terrapin is male or female). Both the coprodeum and urodeum empty into the proctodeum, and from here all faeces and urine are passed out of the vent.

LIVER

The liver is the largest organ inside the body and has many functions. It plays an important part in the breaking down of proteins and fats in food. It also helps the body to get rid of poisons and other harmful substances.

PANCREAS

The pancreas produces juices which help to breakdown food.

PROBLEMS OF THE DIGESTIVE SYSTEM

STOMATITIS

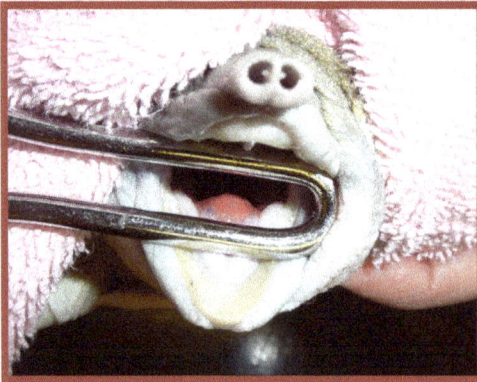

Stomatitis is inflammation of the mouth. It is commonly known as mouth rot. Stomatitis can be caused by either a viral or a bacterial infection. Damage to the mouth can also cause mouth rot.

Pay particular attention to the condition of the house.

Low temperatures in the house can lead to a weakening of the immune system.

Check the furniture in your terrapin's house to make sure that there are no sharp areas which could damage his mouth.

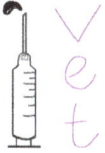

If you think your terrapin has stomatitis get him checked by the vet. He may require help with feeding and some antibiotic treatment.

FATTY LIVER DISEASE

Terrapin with feeding tube

Terrapins need to eat regularly. Fatty liver disease is also known as hepatic lipidosis. Liver cells become swamped with fat, preventing the liver from working properly. It is very difficult to detect fatty liver disease. There are no obvious symptoms but a terrapin with this condition will stop eating. It is important to weigh your terrapin regularly to spot any severe weight loss.

Low temperature can cause loss of appetite.

29

Always feed the right kind of food to your terrapin. Terrapins may like cat food but it is important that they do not eat too much of it. It can make them very ill.

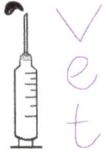

If your terrapin loses more than 10% of his bodyweight you should take him to the vet. He may need an operation that involves fitting a feeding tube to help him to get better.

IMPACTION AND CONSTIPATION

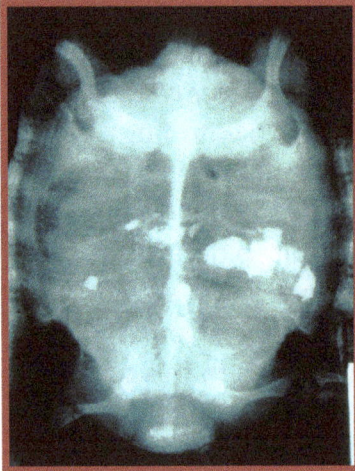

Terrapins often eat material from the floor of their house by mistake. This can lead to impaction in the large intestine. This is when pieces of the material clump together to cause a blockage. Constipation is when a terrapin cannot pass faeces. If your terrapin is constipated you may notice him straining to pass faeces and lifting his shell high off the floor. His faeces may also look very dry.

The temperature in your terrapin's house is vital. If it is too cold the intestines cannot digest food properly and this can lead to constipation.

Calcium is needed to make the intestines work properly. Ensure that your terrapin's UV light is at the correct height and is not too old. The UV light helps the terrapin to absorb calcium through the intestine.

It is very important that your terrapin has water at all times and that the humidity is at the correct level. Dehydration often leads to constipation.

Make sure your terrapin is eating the right type of food and the correct amount.

Make sure that the material you use for the floor of the tank is large enough not to be swallowed by a hungry terrapin.

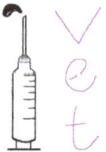

Constipation is often left until it is too late. If an impaction is very severe an operation may be necessary to remove the material blocking the intestine.

A prolapse happens when one of the organs that are plumbed into the vent (for example the large intestine or the bladder) gets pushed out of the body. Egg binding and low calcium in the diet can cause a vent prolapse.

It is very common for male terrapins to push their phallus (willy) through the vent. This is commonly mistaken for a prolapse.

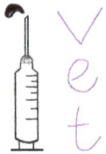

A prolapse is an emergency. If you suspect a prolapse you must take your terrapin to the vet as soon as possible.

LUNGS

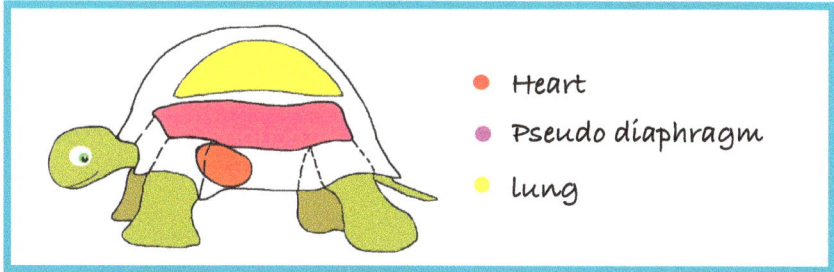

- Heart
- Pseudo diaphragm
- lung

Mammals, lizards and snakes have ribs. The terrapin ribs fused millions of years ago to make his shell. He cannot move his shell to breathe but has developed a clever way of breathing.

Inside the bodies of mammals there is a big sheet of muscle called the diaphragm. This separates the chest, where the lungs are situated, and the abdomen where the stomach and intestines are. This muscle moves in and out all the time when breathing.

Your terrapin has a pseudo diaphragm. It is not a muscle. It is a large sheet of tissue attached to the front and back legs. In order to breathe, he has to pull his legs and his head out very slightly. Watch him and you will see him breathe.

Terrapins are unable to cough. This can be a problem because if they get a build-up of fluid in their lungs, they are unable to clear it by coughing. They have huge spongy lungs that fill up a large part of the space in the shell. The wind pipe or the trachea splits into the bronchi very soon after leaving the back of the throat. This allows the terrapin to pull his head right back into his shell. His neck has an S shape to it. Without this early split in his windpipe he would not be able to breathe when he draws back into his shell to hide.

This is very common in terrapins. It is sometimes caused by a piece of grass or hay becoming stuck inside the nose, but it can also be caused by bacterial and viral infections. Runny Nose can make the terrapin very unwell.

Different terrapins should not be mixed. It is important to think carefully before you consider looking after someone elses terrapin.

Keeping your terrapin at the correct temperature helps to ensure that all the organs are working properly and that his immune system remains healthy.

A balanced diet helps fight off infection.

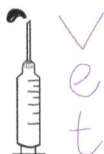

This condition could mean a visit to the vet. Serious infections may need antibiotics or a feeding tube fitting.

34

LUNG PROBLEMS

Pneumonia is the inflammation and infection of the lungs. It is common in terrapins and often develops due to poor housing. Serious lung infections cause the terrapin to stretch their neck and open their mouth, gasping for air.

It is vital that the terrapin's house is kept at the correct temperature with the correct level of humidity.

A good diet protects the immune system.

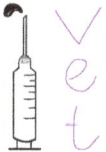

If your terrapin is showing signs of illness then you must take him to the vet. Pneumonia can be vert difficult to treat. Sometimes an operation is needed to treat the lung infection.

HEART

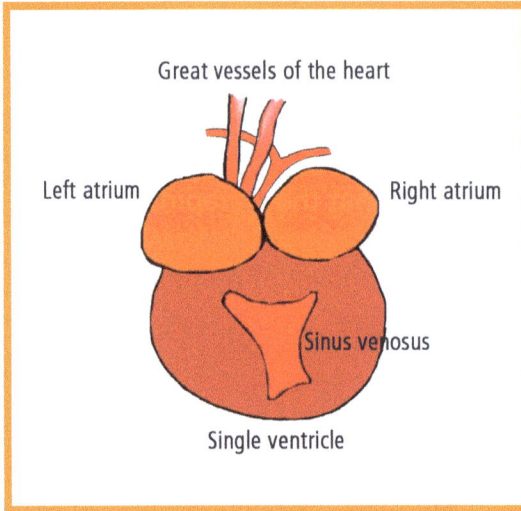

Great vessels of the heart

Left atrium

Right atrium

Sinus venosus

Single ventricle

The heart is a muscle which collects blood full of oxygen from the lungs and pumps it around the body. It also collects blood full of carbon dioxide from the body and pumps it back to the lungs. This cycle goes on continuously.

The heart sits in the chest cavity in mammals and is divided into four chambers. The right atrium collects blood full of carbon dioxide from the body, sends it down to the right ventricle which then pumps it to the lungs. The left atrium collects blood full of oxygen from the lungs, sends it down to the left ventricle which pumps it around the body. Blood is constantly being pumped from right to left, via the lungs and travels around the body inside a series of tubes of varying diameters. These are known as blood vessels.

The heart of a terrapin differs from the heart of a mammal in several ways. It is especially adapted to suit the life of a reptile. It sits between the front legs under the lungs and the pseudo diaphragm. Inside the heart of the terrapin there are three chambers. These are the right atrium, left atrium and the ventricle. There is also an extra chamber outside the heart

Great vessels leaving the heart

Left atrium

Right atrium

Single ventricle and great
vessels leaving the heart

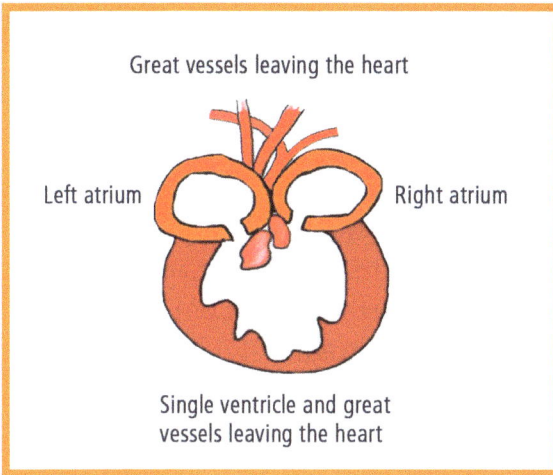

called the sinus venosus which collects blood. Terrapins can move blood to wherever it is needed in the body. Remember how our mammal hearts always pump blood round the body from right to left? Terrapins can change the direction of the blood so that it can flow backwards. This is one of the ways that terrapins can survive if they do not have enough oxygen or if they become dehydrated.

HEART DISEASE

Heart disease is not commonly diagnosed in terrapins. Terrapins with a sick heart will be very quiet and may struggle to breathe.

There are parasites that kill the red blood cells. These are not common in terrapins that are bred in the UK. The parasite causes symptoms that are similar to those of heart failure. These symptoms include swelling of the legs and neck and gasping for breath.

When a house is too cold it can prevent the heart from beating fast enough to keep the blood pumping to all the vital organs.

Having a good balanced diet is essential to maintain a healthy heart.

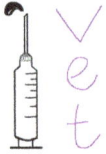

A terrapin with suspected heart disease needs to visit the vet. Treatment might involve medication to support the heart but often these cases are very hard to treat.

REPRODUCTIVE SYSTEM

The reproductive system produces sperm and eggs. Even if your terrapin lives alone the reproductive system is still active and can develop problems.

To determine whether the terrapin is male or female you will need to check the tail length. In general males have longer tails and the vent (bottom) lies outside the shell. Young terrapins can be difficult to sex. Male terrapins also develop a depression in the plastron to enable them to mate with the female terrapin. The plastron is the name for the underside of the shell.

MALES

Male terrapins have two testicles which produce sperm. They are inside the body near the kidneys. The male terrapins have one sex organ called the phallus (willy). This lies inside the vent and is only used for carrying sperm. It does not carry or pass urine.

PHALLUS PROBLEMS

PROLAPSE

The phallus is normally inside the vent and only comes out for mating. If the phallus gets stuck outside the body this is known as a prolapse. A prolapsed phallus can become damaged and infected.

39

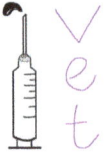

If you think your terrapin has a prolapsed phallus he needs to visit the vet. If the phallus has suffered a lot of damage or has become infected he may need an operation to remove it.

FEMALES

Female terrapins have two ovaries which produce eggs. These are found inside the body near the kidneys. They also have two oviducts. These are tubes along which the eggs are transported to the urodeum area of the vent. Terrapins tend to lay several hard or rubbery eggs (depending on the type of terrapin) at a time. If they susccessfully mate with a male terrapin the eggs will hatch approximately 70-100 days later. However, female terrapins can produce eggs without mating

EGG PROBLEMS

FOLLICULAR STASIS AND EGG BINDING

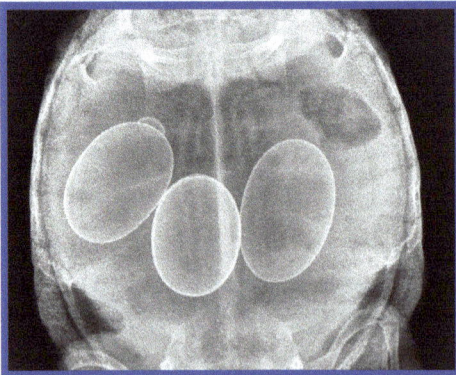

Follicular stasis is a condition which occurs when the eggs do not develop properly and are without a shell. These undeveloped eggs remain inside the body and can make an affected terrapin very ill.

Egg binding is more common in terrapins. In this case the eggs have been made and are fully developed but they become stuck inside the body and cannot be laid. The picture shows an egg bound terrapin.

40

and sometimes this can lead to problems.

The house must be kept at the correct temperature. If it is too cold her body will struggle to make and lay eggs.

Dehydration will make it very difficult for your terrapin to lay eggs.

Making eggs uses a large amount of energy. Ensure that your terrapin has an adequate and balanced diet.

Your terrapin will need a hiding place in her house with plenty of substrate. This allows her to dig holes where she will bury her eggs.

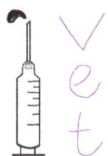

If your terrapin develops any egg related problems she will need to visit the vet. Egg bound terrapins need an operation to remove the retained eggs from the body. Follicular stasis can only be corrected by spaying. This is an operation to remove the ovaries and oviducts.

KIDNEYS

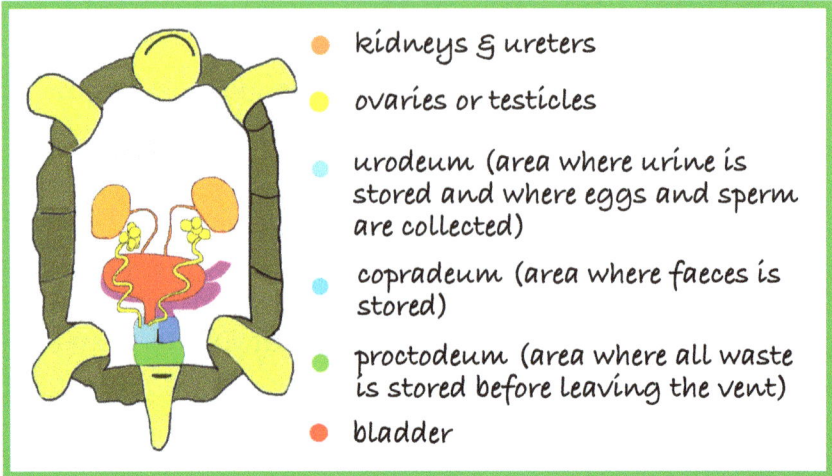

- kidneys & ureters
- ovaries or testicles
- urodeum (area where urine is stored and where eggs and sperm are collected)
- copradeum (area where faeces is stored)
- proctodeum (area where all waste is stored before leaving the vent)
- bladder

Mammals and terrapins have two kidneys. The purpose of the kidneys is to remove poisonous waste material from the body.

THE MAMMAL KIDNEY

All fluid taken in by the body is processed by the kidneys. These include cups of tea, soft drinks and of course water. The kidney ensures that there is enough water to keep the body hydrated. Any water not required is stored in the bladder until it is passed as urine, which is a clear yellow liquid.

THE REPTILE KIDNEY

The kidney of the reptile is different. It does not have the ability to retain water within the body. Most reptiles' urine is a mixture of water and a solid white material called uric acid. The terrapin is different and has developed unique ways to keep his body hydrated. Unlike most land reptiles, terrapins produce urea in the urine rather than uric acid. Urea is clear, similar to urine without the solid white material that is uric acid.

Terrapins are unusual as they have a large bladder connected to the urodeum. It can hold almost a third of their body weight. There is a small flap inside the urodeum that can move water into the large bowel where it is reabsorbed into the body. The terrapin can also suck water up through the vent whilst bathing. Their urine is stored in the urodeum and passes out of the body through the vent.

KIDNEY PROBLEMS

KIDNEY FAILURE

Many different diseases affect the kidneys. These include infections, inflammation, toxic damage and parasites. A terrapin with kidney failure will be less active than usual, lose his appetite, suffer weight loss and become dehydrated.

The house must be at the correct temperature.

Your terrapin always needs access to drinking water.

Correct diet is vital. Do not be tempted to feed cat food to your terrapin. This could damage his kidneys. Do not over dust his food with calcium powder as this can also damage the kidneys. A good diet also helps to support the immune system.

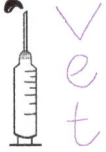

Any weight loss or change in eating habits needs a visit to the vet.

NUTRITIONAL DISEASE

Nutritional diseases are caused by incorrect diet. They can occur if fed too much or too little of the necessary nutrients, vitamins and minerals needed to maintain good health. Nutritional disease is commonly seen in terrapins, yet it is preventable.

MALNUTRITION

Malnutrition is the result of incorrect diet. This can either be too much food or not enough.

A malnourished, starving terrapin

Keeping your terrapin at the correct temperature helps his stomach and small intestine to absorb all the nutrients from his food.

Your terrapin needs a good source of UV light to help his body absorb calcium from the intestine.

Make sure you feed a varied diet to your terrapin.

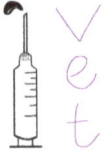

Most cases of malnutrition need veterinary attention.

Terrapin with swollen eyes

Vitamin A is needed to keep the inside of the mouth, the eyes and the kidneys working. Lack of this vitamin can cause thickening of the eyelids as shown in the photograph. It can also lead to kidney failure.

VITAMIN D3 AND CALCIUM DEFICIENCY

This photograph shows the shell sloping at the back. This is because the bone is soft and therefore the stronger muscles are pulling the shell out of shape.

Vitamin D3 and calcium are needed to keep your terrapin's bones strong and his muscles active. An insufficiency will lead to the bones and shell becoming soft and bendy.

 Keeping your terrapin at the correct temperature helps his stomach and small intestine to absorb all the nutrients from his food.

 Your terrapin needs a good source of UV light to help his body absorb calcium from the intestine.

 Make sure you feed a varied diet to your terrapin.

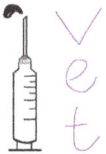 If your terrapin has a nutritional disease he may need to visit the vet for vitamin injections. If the disease is severe the terrapin may require a feeding tube.

PARASITES AND INFECTIOUS DISEASES

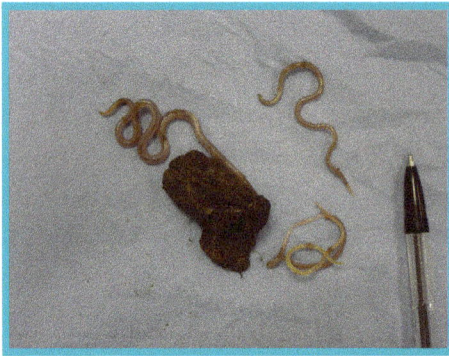

Parasites are creatures that feed off another animal. There are two basic types of parasites. Internal ones live inside the body and external ones live on the outside.

One example of an internal parasite is roundworm as seen in the photograph. Roundworms and tapeworms are found inside the intestines.

Mites and ticks are external parasites that suck the blood and bite the skin.

Terrapins can also have other parasites that live within the blood cells and also the bladder. These parasites are more common in terrapins that have been imported.

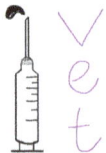

If you see any moving black or red dots on your terrapin's skin, or worms in his faeces, you need to take him to the vet. These are signs of parasites.

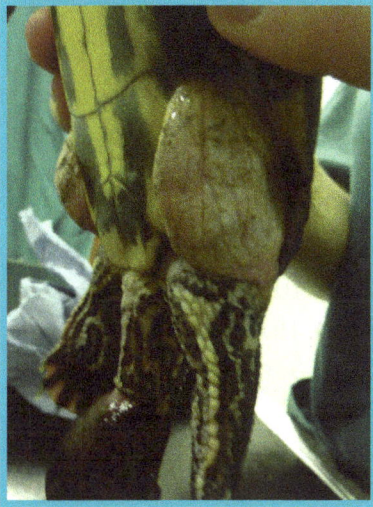

Bacterial infections can cause the skin and the shell to become red and blotchy. This is not common in terrapins but is often very serious if they do develop this condition.

Swollen red skin in the back leg of a terrapin

Keep the house in good condition and make sure it is always at the correct temperature to prevent infection.

Clean water prevents bacteria from breeding. Dirty water can lead to infection.

A good diet promotes an immune system that can fight infection.

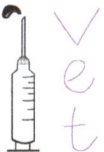

This is a very serious condition and if you think your terrapin is ill you must take him to the vet as soon as possible for antibiotics.

49

GROWTHS

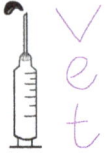

If you find any lump or swelling on your terrapin take him to the vet. To find out exactly what the growth is the vet may need to do some tests. It may be a tumour. Some tumours are types of cancer that can spread. However, the lumps may be abscesses or cysts. Some growths can be surgically removed.

Neurological Disease

The brain and the spinal chord in terrapins are similar to those found in mammals. There are diseases that can affect the nervous system but these are not common.

SKELETON

Terrapins have a special skeleton. The bones have grown together to form a box around the body. Only the head, legs and tail are exposed. When the terrapin is being attacked or is frightened he draws his head, legs and tail into the shell which gives him protection.

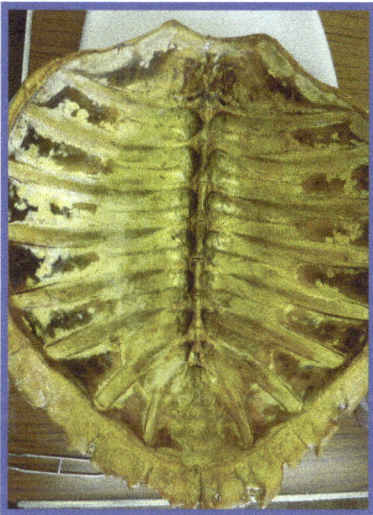

Millions of years ago, the terrapin had ribs. Over time the ribs become flatter and wider until they joined together to make the shell. The shell is made up of bone. On top of the bone are scutes. The bones and the scutes do not lie directly over each other which give the shell extra strength.

The back bone or vertebrae are part of the shell. The carapace is the name for the top part of the shell. The plastron is the name for the underside of the shell.

PYRAMIDING

This is a condition where the shell grows too quickly. Although this is not painful to the terrapin it is thought to be caused by too much protein in the diet or poor incubation before hatching.

CONGENITAL (BIRTH) FAULTS

It is quite common to have terrapins born with imperfections.

Terrapins can have small defects. This shell has a V shape in it.

More serious defects can limit the growth of the terrapin.

The two terrapins are the same age. The small terrapin may not grow any bigger and may have a short life.

INDEX

E

egg binding 31, 40
eggs 27, 42
exothermic 9
external parasites 48
eyelids 22, 23, 24, 46

F

faeces 27, 42
fatty liver disease 29
feeding tube 29, 30, 34, 47
follicular stasis 40

G

growth 14, 50, 52

H

heart 10, 36, 37, 38
hepatic lipidosis 29
hibernate 5
hibernation 5
humidity 2, 12
hygrometer 12
hypovitaminosis a 24

I

impaction and constipation 30
insurance 4, 5
intestines 10, 11, 26, 30, 33, 48
iris 22

K

kidney failure 43, 46
kidneys 42

S

salmonella 1
scleral ossicles 23
scud = septicaemic cutaneous ulcerative disease 20
scute 14
shedding (ecdysis) 15
sinus venosus 37
skeleton V, 51
skin V, 14, 16, 18
sperm 27, 42
spinal chord 50
stomach 27
stomatitis 28

T

tapeworms 48
testicles 42
ticks 48
trachea 33
trauma 19
tumour 50

U

ulcer 24
uric acid 42, 43
urine 27, 42
urodeum 27, 42
uv light 2, 11, 18, 20, 25, 30, 45, 47

V

vent 26, 27, 31, 32, 39, 40, 42, 43, 54
ventricle 36
vitamin a 46
vitamin d3 11, 14, 18

W

willy 32, 39
wind pipe 33

Lightning Source UK Ltd.
Milton Keynes UK
UKHW02f1256060818
326825UK00007B/132/P

9 780957 656864